D0993612

WILD IN THE CITY

A celebration of the open spaces of Putney, Barnes & Richmond

For Diana – my lovely wife and best friend

Welcome to my first book of photography

We are extremely fortunate living where we do, in the south west corner of London, surrounded by many areas of beautiful open space – much of it free to visit. I have always enjoyed walking, and since bringing a lively springer spaniel into the family in 2006, it has given me the perfect excuse to do more. I am also very fond of photography and I have been lucky enough to combine my hobbies by taking my camera along when we go for our walks. This book is as much a diary of those walks, as a book of my favourite images. Most of the pictures were taken after January 2009, when I bought my new digital SLR camera.

I have split my book up into the five main areas that we walk (although it should be noted that for obvious reasons dogs are not allowed into the Wetland Centre).

Again, for simplicity, I have tried to feature my pictures chronologically and each section starts with pictures from the beginning of the year and moves through spring into summer.

To help you try and place where we are in each section I was pleased to get the help of local artist, Julianna Franchetti, who provided some lovely watercolour maps of each area. These are not intended to be perfect facsimiles, so please use them more as a guide.

I hope you enjoy your journey through my pictures, as much as I enjoyed taking them and that it inspires you to make more of the beautiful countryside that we have around us.

In compiling my book I am indebted to many people for their help and I would like to thank the following:

My wife and family; my mum for helping with the funding; Pam and Gerry for some superior proofing; Julianna Franchetti for the illustrations; Nick Cobb from the Putney School of Art & Design; my new photography friends – in particular, Katie, Zeenya and Rachelle; Isla Dawes from the Barnes Bookshop and my graphic designer, Steve Gibson.

Pat Pritchard and Daniel Hearsum from the Royal Parks, who kindly gave me permission to take and use pictures from Richmond and Bushy Park; Gordon Vincent and the other rangers from the Putney & Wimbledon Conservators, who also gave me permission to use pictures from their area.

Reg Leach from Richmond Council's environmental office, who authorised the use of pictures from the Leg o' Mutton and Stasa Veroukis from WWT London Wetland Centre, who gave me permission to use pictures from the Wetland Centre.

Andrew Wilson
London, 2009

My constant companion, Josie – our springer spaniel

My usual mode of transport – my wife's Smart. She has taken up cycling to work, which leaves me this fun, little car to drive.

If you're a local resident you'll have seen plenty of these cheeky birds commandeering the trees of Richmond Park

Putney Bridge by local artist, Julianna Franchetti

CONTENTS

Barnes Common

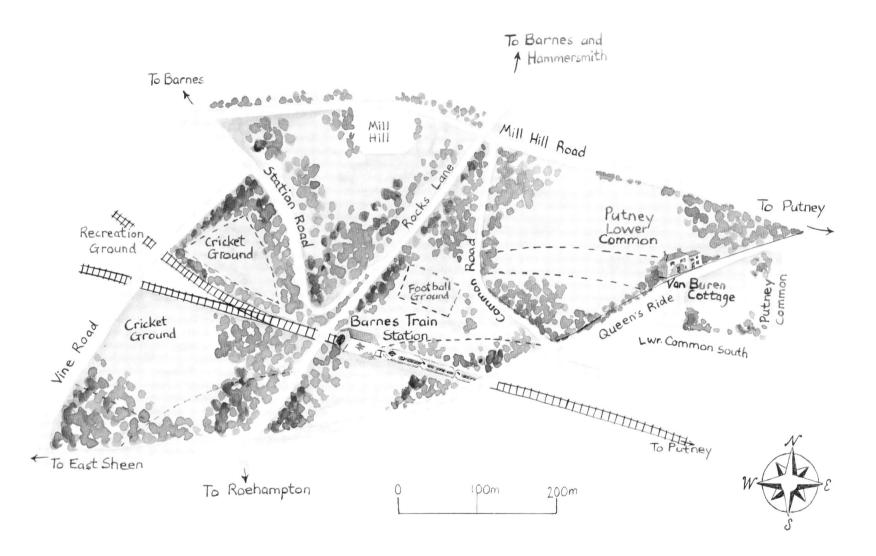

To Barnes and
↑ Hammersmith

To Barnes ↗

Mill Hill

Mill Hill Road

To Putney →

Station Road

Rocks Lane

Putney Lower Common

Recreation Ground

Cricket Ground

Common Road

Van Buren Cottage

Putney Common

Vine Road

Cricket Ground

Football Ground

Barnes Train Station

Queen's Ride

Lwr. Common South

← To East Sheen

↓ To Roehampton

To Putney

0   100m   200m

N
W   E
S

The village of Barnes can trace its history back over 1000 years, when the land was granted to The Dean and Chapter of St Paul's by the King. With the distinctive loop in the river, it was long regarded as a remote and inaccessible place, until the construction of Hammersmith Bridge in 1827 and the arrival of the railway in 1847. With the subsequent development, the last vestiges of rural life and the dominant local industry – market gardening – disappeared.

With thanks to the Barnes & Mortlake History Society for the background information

Illustration Julianna Franchetti

The big freeze

In February 2009, London saw more snow than had been seen in a generation and Barnes was transformed.

The path across the common and the football pitch by the station became unrecognisable; good fun though, because the schools were closed and making snowmen replaced lessons for a few days.

The first signs of spring

Gorse

A fox taking in the first
rays of warm sunshine
beside Barnes station

Snowdrops

Crocus

Dwarf iris

Quince

Cherry blossom on Church Road, Barnes

Pussy willow

Pussy willow

Cherry blossom

Horse chestnut

These lovely little wild garlic
flowers spring up all over the
woods besides Ranelagh Avenue

Bluebells — which are not always blue

Clematis

Speckled wood butterfly

Honesty

Greater celandine

Blackthorn blossom

The leaves of the horse chestnut (bottom left) are spectacular at this time of year. It is such a shame that these majestic giants are under increasing attack from a mining moth, which has apparently spread here from Asia.

The larvae literally eat the leaves from the inside, eventually killing them. Although the leaves grow back the following year, this annual attack is taking its toll and many trees are now dying. Witness some of them around the cricket pitch by Barnes Station (see the tree in the centre of the picture bottom right).

The first recorded sighting of the moth was close by in Wimbledon in 2002. It is now The Royal Horticultural Society's number one pest. There are so many horse chestnuts in Greater London that if the toll increases, our landscape will change completely. For instance – just consider the effect this will have on the lovely avenues of trees in Bushy Park – conker fights may become a thing of the past.

The insects that can be found in large numbers beneath sycamore leaves are obviously territorial. It cannot be mere coincidence that they are so evenly spaced.

The silhouette of a fly under an oak tree leaf

This family of foxes set up home in the woods beside Barnes Station

Some of the seeds of the
sycamore tree turn a lovely
pink colour in June

Broom seed pods, which turn
black before popping open and
ejecting their contents

The path from the football pitch
walking towards Queens Ride.
This small corner of the common
is left very much alone.
For instance – no mowing takes
place and the grasses and wild
flowers grow very tall.

A female stag beetle. South west London, with all its wide open spaces, is fortunate in that this threatened creature has been able to thrive, whereas elsewhere it has lost much of its natural habitat. Wood is now left where it has fallen, rather than being cleared away, to encourage creatures such as these, whose young rely on rotting wood and vegetation to live.

This beautiful red admiral still seemed able to fly despite having a piece of his wing missing

A peacock butterfly feasting
on some buddleia down
beside Barnes station

Wild teasel

Bumble bees *love* lavender!

The map illustration shows the following labels:

- Chiswick Eyot
- Ferry Lane
- To Hammersmith Bridge
- Verdun Road
- The Towpath
- Fisherman's Place
- Nature Reserve
- The Harrodian School
- River Thames
- Suffolk Road
- Lonsdale Road
- Gerard Road
- Nassau Road
- To Barnes
- N W E S
- 0 100m 200m
- ▬ – road
- ▬ – cycle/footpath

Leg o' Mutton Nature Reserve

The Leg o' Mutton derives its name from its distinctive shape and is one of Barnes' hidden gems. However, it may never have existed, had it not been for the timely intervention, in the late 1950s, of some notable local people who stepped in and persuaded the council to stop the local waterboard selling the then reservoir for development.

With a temporary reprieve, further work was done locally to uphold this decision and in the late '60s two local artists came up with the inspired idea of turning it into a nature reserve, which was accepted.

Since then, the area has become a wildlife haven, prompting Richmond Council in 1990 to designate it one of their Local Nature Reserves, lending it status and long term protection. The council and local people are to be congratulated for their foresight in saving such a beautiful area and for their continued support.

The reserve in the 1960s before development (by an unknown photographer)

*With thanks to Catherine Sacre, Susan Gibson and Sally Holloway from **Barnes in Common** (the magazine for Barnes churches) – the source of the background on the Leg o' Mutton*

***Illustration** Julianna Franchetti*

A fox caught late one evening down amongst
the reed beds, looking fit and healthy

Top Reed bed ***Above*** Buttercups

Clouds of midges in the late evening sun

The ringed-neck parakeets love the wych elm seeds that appear in the spring. There are many of these on the river side of the reservoir and the parakeets are so pre-occupied eating that they will tolerate visitors getting quite close.

Great crested grebe

Plane tree flowers

I am most grateful to a friend of mine, Angela, who early in 2009 tipped me off as to the whereabouts of several birds of prey in the Leg o' Mutton Reserve. She kindly told me where these young tawny owls had last been seen. Unbelievably, as I crept through the undergrowth, with Josie on a lead beside me, they were still there.

26

Elder

Maple overhanging the lake

Bladder campion

Some new spring arrivals – mallard chicks

Speckled wood butterfly

Cabbage white butterfly

Above Hover fly feeding on a thistle
Right (top to bottom) Looking west along the reserve towards Barnes and the river; A family of coots feeding in the water; A flock of parakeets

A lot of the benches that exist around the lake have some mark or other and I rather like this one

Hogweed

A pair of kestrels have nested in the same hole almost every year for several years. Within minutes of my friend telling me about them, I was able to take the picture on the left – but I had to stand for two hours to get the picture opposite. It is sometimes just a matter of timing.

On the next such occasion, I must remember to bring along something to eat and drink.

Top Wild cherry
Above By the state of his feathers, this young robin has a little growing up to do yet

A pair of sparrowhawks also inhabit the reserve and regularly nest. I believe these to be pictures of the female.

The handbooks show the male with a white band above its eyes, but they also show both with it. They had two chicks this year, which appear to have fledged successfully.

Speckled wood butterfly

Red admiral butterfly

One of the many herons that frequent the reserve, standing on one of the floating islands

One of the pair of mute swans that claims territorial rights over the reserve. Although they nested this year on the bank of the reservoir, and sat for ages, none of the eggs hatched. They were either very unlucky or lacked parenting skills.

Insects love buddleia – as the painted lady and cabbage
white butterflies, and the hover fly, clearly show

King's Mere Lake, near Tibbetts Corner

Putney Heath & Wimbledon Common

Wimbledon and Putney commons (including Putney Lower Common) cover an area of over 1100 acres and exist today in their present form through an Act of Parliament passed in 1871.

Prior to this date, the land belonged to the Lord of the Manor, who granted various 'common rights' to a select number of local tenants. Thankfully, the act saved the land for future generations to enjoy and saw the management of the area pass to a body of convervators, five elected and three appointed, funded by a small levy on local people. This has ensured that an area of natural beauty has remained open, unenclosed, unbuilt on and its natural aspect preserved.

The local residents that made it all possible back in the 19th century should be congratulated for their foresight, long before it became fashionable to protect our wide open spaces.

Background information courtesy of the Ranger's Office and the Commons Information Centre which can be found next to the windmill (www.wpcc.org.uk)

Illustration Julianna Franchetti

A heron is disturbed beside the small pond by the top of Roehampton Vale. This pond, like many others in the parks, struggles to retain its water in the summer and regularly dries up. The heathland opposite tends to flood in the winter, but again, dries up in the summer.

The first signs of spring

Young sycamore leaves
can look spectacular
when light is reflected
through them – as these
I found in the woods
near Scio Pond

White cherry blossom

Morning dew

One misty, April morning at King's Mere

Within a couple of hours the mist had lifted

The windmill in the
middle of the common
looked stunning as the
sun shone on it whilst
a storm was brewing
all around

The family of mute swans on Queen's Mere

After problems in 2008, the rangers organised a new, larger, floating raft for the swans to nest on – which was a touch of genius. No sooner had it arrived than they made it their home, with fantastic results.

The windmill on the common

This was some peculiar behaviour I witnessed, where a couple of
coots were attacking something in the water. I didn't discover what,
but they clearly felt very strongly about it.

Autumn colours on Queen's Mere

Beverley Brook

Bracken in the woods

The nature trail in the woods beside the windmill

Young moorhens

Scio Pond

Off the top of Roehampton Lane, where it meets Roehampton Vale.

This heron regularly likes to perch here and it always makes me chuckle. The fishing is clearly very good for him and I suppose leg irons would only be appropriate if he actually used a rod and line.

Female tufted duck at the gravel pit

Left There is a path that cuts right through the middle of the Royal Wimbledon golf course and very pretty it is too, with wonderful views either side. **Above** This pond is called the Bluegate Gravel Pit. Despite the rain in July 2009, it has unfortunately dried up again. Let's hope there is sufficient rain in the autumn and winter to re-fill it.

Tree fungus

Blackthorn berries

A common garden spider

Fallow deer

Richmond Park

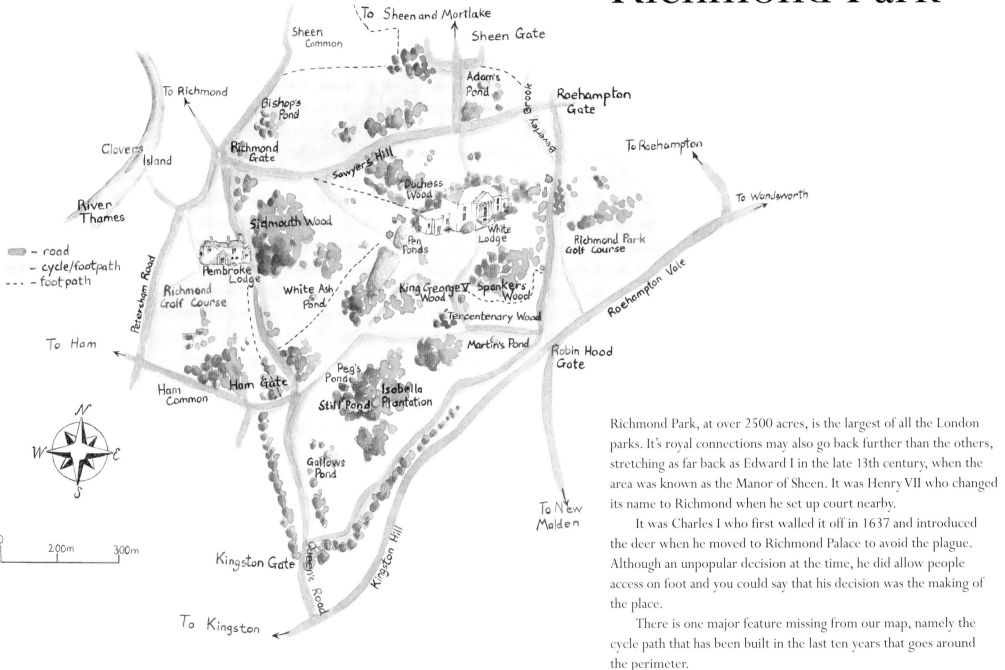

Richmond Park, at over 2500 acres, is the largest of all the London parks. It's royal connections may also go back further than the others, stretching as far back as Edward I in the late 13th century, when the area was known as the Manor of Sheen. It was Henry VII who changed its name to Richmond when he set up court nearby.

It was Charles I who first walled it off in 1637 and introduced the deer when he moved to Richmond Palace to avoid the plague. Although an unpopular decision at the time, he did allow people access on foot and you could say that his decision was the making of the place.

There is one major feature missing from our map, namely the cycle path that has been built in the last ten years that goes around the perimeter.

With thanks to the Royal Parks website for the information here

Illustration Julianna Franchetti

Winter arrived with an unusually heavy fall of snow in February 2009. Great for the fun seekers, because schools were closed and everyone headed for the parks.

Tercentenary Wood, near the approach to the car park for Pen Ponds

The pair of mute swans on the smaller of the two Pen Ponds

Red deer

Beverley Brook

Josie in the larger Pen Pond

A damp log steaming in the
winter sunshine

A Canadian goose over the ponds

The pair of mute swans on the smaller of the two Pen Ponds, one beautiful February morning

Pen Ponds – late one February afternoon

The first signs of spring

Horse chestnut tree buds

Ring-necked parakeet

Crocus

The view west from the top of the hill near Ham

**A glorious show of
daffodils up through
Prince Charles spinney**

February gold

Actaea

Kilworth

February gold

Martin's Pond, on the approach to the car park at Pen Ponds

An Egyptian goose making
good use of the facilities at
Martin's Pond

Larch tree cones

Above Birch catkins ***Below*** Hornbeam catkins

Fallen cherry blossom on water

Bracken

Cherry

Beech tree

Dusk over Spankers Hill

Dusk over Pen Ponds

One of the many horse rides to be found all over the park

The year's offspring from the pair of Egyptian geese to be found at Martin's Pond. Unlike last year when they raised all their young, some tragedy befell them this year and within the first few days they lost four of their seven goslings. Presumably scared, they soon moved the remaining three to Pen Ponds.

Morning sunshine
in the woods

The Martin's Pond
geese before they
left for Pen Ponds

Maple

Magnolia

Benches can be found all over the park and besides the odd goose (page 67), can offer the human visitor a wonderful vantage point from which to admire the view

Do *you* have a favourite?

Still Pond

The Isabella Plantation

This feature of the park, so spectacular particularly in April and May when all the blossom is out, can trace its roots back to at least 1831, when Lord Sidmouth, as the deputy park ranger, started transforming it into what we know today.

It was he who fenced it off from the rest of the park and gave the area its name — a name that may be derived from the colour of the soil found in this part of the park. The beautiful trees and shrubs date from the 1950s, when the then park superintendent and his chief gardener planted the azaleas and rhododendrons.

The plantation's unique importance to nature has been recognised by being declared an area of Special Scientific Interest.

Rhododendron

Magnolia

Above Camellia ***Below*** Rhododendron

Mandarin duck (male)

Above Mandarin duck (female) *Below* Rhododendron

A great variety of heathers can also be found in the plantation

Young moorhen

Above Thomson's Pond *Below* Noble fir tree cones

A young and very inquisitive Mandarin duck

Rhododendron

From May each year these banded demoiselle damselflies can be found in large numbers all over the park, wherever there is water. The males are blue and females green.

Pen Ponds

Swans are fiercely territorial and this pair is no exception (also seen so majestically on page 63). They may look resplendent and wonderful parents, but they scare the living daylights out of any goose that dares to set foot on their lake (the smaller of the two). These Egyptian geese were attacked, but successfully protected their young and no-one was harmed on this occasion.

One evening in May

Ham Cross plantation

Coronation plantation

Sunlit cobwebs

Starlings flock in large numbers to feed, swooping in and out of the grass

Oak trees in the late evening sun

Rabbits

Sawyer's Hill

Small copper butterfly

The City of London from the hill

Small copper and meadow brown butterflies

Gotcha! This poor copper's been nicked

Pen Ponds through King George V's Wood at dusk

The one good thing about poor
weather is you can sometimes witness
the most glorious cloud formations
(left) – looking east towards Sheen
Gate one day in late July

Deer

There are over 650 deer within Richmond Park. They are the main reason it is a park at all, having been a deer hunting area back in the time of the Tudors and Stuarts. They are responsible for the distinctive look of the park, with the way in which they graze and the 'browse line' they create in the trees. The birds on their backs are tolerated as they help to keep down the parasites.

White Ash Pond near Pembroke Lodge

Drinking in Martin's Pond

It should be remembered that the deer are wild animals and should be approached with care, especially in early summer when they have young and in the autumn, during the rut

The adult crows can be comic, as shown by this one rifling the bins

I stumbled across this poor young crow (right) in the grass one day in early June and wondered why there was such a commotion from its relatives.

I soon discovered why – as they took turns to dive-bomb the fox (above), who was hiding in the grass trying to get this fledgling, and others that were littered around. Thwarted by a fence, the fox failed with this one, but soon caught another and raced off.

A young magpie

An extraordinary feat of nature is the way that caterpillars transform themselves into butterflies and moths.

These striking orange/yellow caterpillars (left) of the cinnabar moth (right), are found throughout the summer voraciously feeding on ragwort, which is poisonous for grazing animals.

It was to control ragwort that these caterpillars were introduced into this country. Cleverly, both the caterpillar and the adult moth can cope with the toxins, hence the bright colours to warn potential predators.

There are few cattle in the park, but the rangers still like to control ragwort for the sake of the horses. The cinnabar is not the only insect that likes ragwort – see the butterflies on page 104.

Red deer late one evening in King George V's Plantation near Pen Ponds

A wren protecting its fledgling (right)

Ham Gate Pond

A heron stalking its breakfast

The longest day at Pen Ponds

Pembroke Lodge

Pembroke Lodge is named after the Countess of Pembroke, who was granted the small house, as it was then, by George III in 1780. Its other claim to fame is that in 1847 Queen Victoria granted it to her new Prime Minister, Lord John Russell — being the younger son of the Duke of Bedford he had no place of his own.

Apparently, because he disliked London so much, most of the business of running the country was conducted here, including cabinet meetings. The lodge has a fabulous view westwards, boasts a restaurant and can now be hired for functions, such as weddings. A brand new information centre was also added in the re-development.

Yarrow

Two great spotted woodpeckers

Looking across Pen Ponds towards White Lodge, which can just be seen behind the trees on the left

One of the many mushrooms that appear in high summer

Above Moon rising over Richmond Park golf course ***Below*** Tercentenary Wood

Pair of nesting ring-necked parakeets

As with the cinnabar moth caterpillars on page 97, these beautiful gatekeeper butterflies (above and right) gather to enjoy the flowers of the ragwort. It was fun to find so many all in one place.

Meadow brown butterfly

A glorious sunrise near Roehampton Gate

Buttercups in the late evening sunshine

Heron

Looking towards Sheen from the woods beside White Lodge

Starlings in the grass amongst the deer by Pen Ponds

Fallow deer in Bone Copse, near White Lodge

A red deer hind and her faun

Bushy Park

A smaller version of Richmond Park with its deer and lakes, Bushy Park lies north of Hampton Court Palace and was established for hunting by Henry VIII. During World War II, Dwight Eisenhower, not wishing to be in central London, made Bushy Park his supreme HQ.

Herons clearly can't read, but to be fair he obviously feels he has certain rights – it *is* called Heron Lake

Coot

One of the famous avenues of trees

WWT London Wetland Centre & Putney Lower Common

The map shows the following labels:

To Hammersmith Bridge

Harrods Village

London Wetland Centre

Castelnau

Towpath

Queen Elizabeth Walk

Tennis Courts

Tennis Courts

Boat House

River Thames

Barn Elms

To Barnes Bridge

Rocks Lane

Running Track

Beverley Brook

Rocks Lane Tennis Centre

Old Barnes Cemetery

Putney Lower Common

To Barnes

Putney Cemetery

Putney Hospital

To Roehampton

Lower Richmond Road

To Putney

Map legend:
- road
- cycle/footpath
- footpath

Scale: 100m 200m

N W E S

The Wildfowl & Wetlands Trust (WWT) which was founded in 1946 by Sir Peter Scott, is one of the UK's leading conservation organisations and works both in the UK and all over the world in support of wetlands for wildlife and people.

Picture with kind permission of Berkeley Homes

The WWT London Wetland Centre covers over 100 acres of what was originally four Victorian reservoirs (see the picture above). The centre is a truly magical place and the three main organisations, WWT, Thames Water and Berkeley Homes, who are behind its creation in 2000 should be congratulated for their vision.

In 2002 the centre was recognized as a Site of Special Scientific Interest. Open to the public seven days a week, all year round, bar Christmas Day, the centre supports a variety of animals and over 180 different bird species.

Illustration Julianna Franchetti

There are plenty of vantage points from which to admire the flora and fauna. However, I did find this wonderful display of daisies beside the car park before I even entered the centre.

The tufted duck and its chicks had just run across the path in front of me before swimming off in formation.

Purple irises

Plants have been encouraged to grow on the roofs of the hides, like the one above. The centre boasts a great variety of birds, which, given its close proximity to London, is quite unique.

Marsh frogs (top) are not native to this country. They may have been introduced from Europe in the 1930s.

A heron hiding in the reeds

During the summer, the centre has the occasional late night opening. When visiting one night in July, hoping to experience a beautiful sunset over the reservoir, I found rain instead.

It did create a photographic moment, though, with an extraordinary dark line being formed by the clouds on the horizon (right). As we left, we found a mallard mother protecting her young (left), which by the look of it were getting a bit old for this. There are at least four chicks that you can see, with more behind and underneath.

Early one day in June, I was fortunate to capture the tufted duck (below) and her chicks running between the ponds.

Putney Lower Common

Bind weed

The old cemetery

Below should be a four-spotted chaser (judging by the markings on its back) but it seems to have only one spot on each wing, which suggests that it might be a broad-bodied chaser

Ladybird on a stinging nettle

Dandelions

Come June, come the snails. On the right you can see the white-lipped and brown-lipped varieties.

On the far right are grave stones of the old cemetery, amongst which was the startled robin below.

Walking around the neighbourhood as I do, I am always upset by the amount of litter there is but you could say that bottom middle (the picture of Beverley Brook) is at least litter with a message.

It is amazing to think that the dark, little monsters on the left take about two weeks to turn into beautiful peacock butterflies like this one. They are pictured feeding on stinging nettles – which is why naturalists are always suggesting that we leave a little wildness in our gardens for plants such as these.

You might think these were oak leaves in the autumn, but they are, in fact, new spring growth

I love the way that these grasses catch the wind

Above Common darter *Below* Large skipper butterfly

Painted lady butterfly

Bindweed – invasive but very pretty

Canadian geese taking off over the playing fields at Barn Elms

Sweet horse chestnuts, a source of food for a great variety of animals from squirrels to deer.

Colophon

Acknowledgements

I am indebted to numerous books, my in-laws, family and friends, Trott (one of my oldest friends and a demon gardener) and to Google in particular, for helping me name some of the plants and insects that I have photographed throughout the year.

I have used *The Wild Flower Key* from Warne Books, *The Collins Complete Guide to British Wild Flowers*, *The Collins Complete Guide to British Trees*, *The Royal Horticultural Society's Gardeners' Encyclopedia*, *The Concise Guide to Butterflies & Moths* and *The Concise Guide to Insects* from Parragon and *The Bumper Book of Nature* from Random House.

I currently use a Canon 450D with a telephoto lens. 2009 was my first foray into the use of a digital SLR and great fun it was, too.

About Julianna Franchetti

Julianna studied at Central St Martins London, obtaining an MA(Hons) after which she worked as an animator/director and background artist for television and film.

Julianna now produces oils and watercolours, many to commission. She holds enthusiastic privately tutored classes in watercolour techniques at her studio in Putney for beginners or painters who need to 'brush up' on their skills. She tutors at several London locations, including Putney School of Art and The Hurlingham Club, and each year runs a fantastic painting holiday in Andalucia, Spain. Julianna exhibits in several galleries and regularly holds successful open studio weekends in Putney where the public can view and purchase her work.
www.juliannafranchetti.co.uk

Production notes

Designed by Steve Gibson
www.thisisgibson.com

Built using QuarkXPress 8
www.quark.com

Colour management by The Missing Horse Consultancy with special thanks to Paul Sherfield
www.missinghorsecons.co.uk

Printed by Pensord with special thanks to Tony Jones
www.pensord.co.uk

Bound by Folio Print Finishing (Bristol) with special thanks to Andy Bird
www.foliobristol.co.uk

Paper supplied by Denmaur Independent Papers with special thanks to Nick Gee
www.denmaur.com

FSC The text papers are 170gsm Symphony Gloss and the cover is 350gsm Symphony Silk. The paper is FSC accredited, which is an assurance that it is sourced from well managed forests and that the producers follow a set of strict guidelines with respect to social and environmental matters.

Published by Andrew Wilson of Unity Print & Publishing, 18 Dungarvan Avenue, London SW15 5QU. Tel: +44 (0)20 8487 2199
www.unity-publishing.co.uk

All rights reserved. No part of this publication may be reproduced, stored in any retrieval system or transmitted in any form or by any means, electronic, mechanical photocopying or otherwise without the prior permission of the copyright holders. Whilst every care has been taken in the production of this book, no responsibility can be accepted for any errors or omissions. The publisher has taken all reasonable care in compiling this work but cannot accept responsibility for the information derived from third parties, which has been taken in good faith.

©2009 Unity Print & Publishing Ltd

Order prints from *Wild in the City*

If you'd like any of the images in this book as personalised prints, cards and much more, please visit our website where you can order from a range of Andrew Wilson's photographs.
www.wildinthecity.co.uk